THE ADVENTURES OF US

A keepsake journal of where we've been
and where we want to go...

Books With Soul™
Somewhere in the desert, sea and forest.
bookswithsoul.com
∞

ISBN 9781949325195

For::

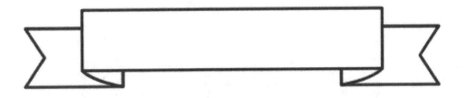

If you want
to preserve
your
memories
you can.

Date we started exploring:

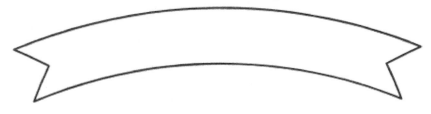

Inside these pages: The Adventures of Us.

I dare you.

Let's travel
the world
together.

Travel, the one thing you buy that makes you richer
-unknown

Let's get rich together!

We can go wherever we want to go.
We will explore this world together.

This travel journal ONLY works if you use it!

Take the time on your excursions or when you return from a fantastic vacation, to record the dates of EVERY trip, journey and adventure together.

This is a book to scribble in, crinkle the pages and write your travel thoughts. A book to take with you, wherever you go, and have it in a physical form for years to come. A book to collect memories, that will last forever.

A book to share and remember. Write in the travel log portion in the back of the book, before you unpack.

THE ADVENTURES OF US

Go. See. Do. Remember.
Figure out where you want to make memories together.
Take the time to record every road trip, vacation, weekend getaway
and anniversary trip.
Collect and preserve your memories.

Section 1:

A section to complete together. Explore how alike or different your
travel preferences are by taking a travel quiz and answering some
prompts and questions. It's okay to enjoy different kinds of
adventures. Introduce your mate to another side of traveling and
you both will grow together.
How well do you know our planet? Do you know the names of all
the countries? Continents?
Create individual and couple bucket lists.

Section 2:

Keep a Master list of every country and continent you visit together.
Make it a habit, and soon you will fill the pages of this book with
treasured memories. Remember where you stayed, dates and
favorite memories.

Introduction:

This book is for YOUR journey as a couple.

The places the two of you will explore in your lifetime.

Where do you want to go? What do you want to see?

The world is yours to traverse, the planet spins as do your ideas together, and there are so many choices of places to stop and get off.

Allow me to be the first to congratulate you both.

Congratulations.

Congratulations on being together and planning together.

Congratulations on having a book to keep track of every vacation, adventure, and journey you will experience together.

As a couple you are way ahead of most of the world. You're creating a collection of memories on paper. A book you will look back to when you can't remember what year you took that cruise, or stayed in the rustic cabin with no heat in the mountains. All your favorite destinations and memories will be in one place.

Sharing ideas and fantasy locations can only add to your enriched life.

Writing things down with pen or pencil, will help both of you see your dreams and inspirations clearly in life. I believe there is something empowering about looking at words, words that only existed in your thoughts, in printed or cursive form. Better yet, thoughts you took the time to share with each other.

I always loved the quote, "If you don't know where you are going, how will you know when you get there?" It's true, we often need a road map of where we are headed, and yet sometimes, it's the journey getting to our designated point that ends up changing our lives. Sometimes it's sharing these ideas with each other.

It doesn't matter when you begin your vacations together. Maybe you just met, or you have been together forever. Maybe you are engaged or have pledged your life to each other.

Honeymoon? A perfect place to take a few moments out of every new day together, to explore your future travel plans and destinations.

It doesn't matter when you start this adventure, it only matters that you began this journey together.

Where do you want to go? What do you want to see?

Some folks desire to see every state in
the United States, or every country in Europe,
South America, Africa, or Asia. Some might have a list of
local places they have never taken the time or
energy to see.

There are no wrong answers.

This book is about what you both want to see and sharing
your ideas.

You may have very different top ten lists, and that is great.
How magnificent to explore each other's hope and dreams
together. On the following pages, take some time to answer
a few questions and create a travel bucket list. Record
both your answers. Write all the ideas you share and
don't share.

In this book, there are no rules. You can create your travel
bucket list, add to it, or delete from it. You are in charge
and you can change it as many times as you like.

So where do you want to go?

Maybe you want to touch every continent. There are either
7 or 8 total continents on this planet and 195 countries
depending on which school of thought you subscribe to.
United Nations currently records 193 countries as
members, and 2 observer states, so I'll go with 195.

I'm going with the 7 continents of the world as: **North A merica, South A merica, A ntarctica, Europe, Asia, Africa and A ustralia.**

As of right now, I have three continents to go to fulfill my goal of touching every continent but loads of countries to visit. I've been fortunate to travel often, and a few years ago I logged over 99 vacations in three years. I even wrote a book about how I was able to plan and afford my journey. _Travel Secrets: An Insider guide to planning, affording and taking more vacations._ So be sure to check the book out to learn how to afford your list. It's free on Kindle Unlimited.

But, the purpose of this book is to make your lists and record your vacations. Where do you want to go? Where do you want to go together?

So, where do you want to go?

This is a journal to not only record and keep a list of travels, but also to help you figure out what destinations **you** most desire to explore. Where does your heart or your mind escape to when you have that moment of peace? What have you been longing to see up close? Maybe it's around the corner, or far away. There are no right answers.
It's a big world out there and the list of possibilities of places to explore are endless.

The back part of this book is to keep a log of your travels. Trust me you think you will remember but you won't.

Write them down before you unpack your suitcase or backpack.

Write down each and every vacation, weekend getaway or adventure you take in a year, a decade, and in your life. List the date, location, where you stayed and a few sentences to describe what you most want to remember. Even if it's one word, I bet ten years you will remember why you wrote that one word.

You might want to share them with your family or friends. Or leave this journal for your parents, children, future children or grandchildren, best friend or closest companions.

Or, perhaps just keep it for yourself, with a cord tied around it, and see how many bucket items you can achieve.
Check the boxes.
Write ideas on the journal pages.

Cross out the names and places you visited, write the date you traveled beside the names on your list.

Write in this book, sketch, doodle, scribble, do what you wish. Paste photos of places you long to go. Pictures you ripped out of a magazine. Carry it in the rain, bend the pages, rip a few out—just do what you want.

It doesn't matter, there are no rules.
Just take more vacations together.

We live in a remarkable era of technology –
and because of this travel has never been easier, more accessible or more affordable.

We only have ourselves to blame for not planning
more time-off to visit the destinations that are
alive in our mind. And, not knowing the destinations
that exist in your other half's mind.

Take the time in your life to figure out your
Travel Bucket List, and your dream destinations.
Then... get busy making it happen.

If you can dream it, it can happen.

EXPLORE and take notes, so you can have a
written history of your adventures.

The first step of a living your travel dreams,
is knowing where and what they are.
Create a road map and set goals.

If you want to travel more,
figure out where.

This is a place for your dreams and
by writing it down,
you are on the road to achieving it.

"The world is a book and those who do not travel read only one page." –

<u>St. Augustine</u>

Let's hold hands and see the world.
List a few of your
Dream Destinations

_____
_____
_____
_____
_____
_____
_____
_____
_____
_____
_____
_____

Ideas

Section 1:
where you've been
and where you want to go.
Creating your Travel Bucket List together.

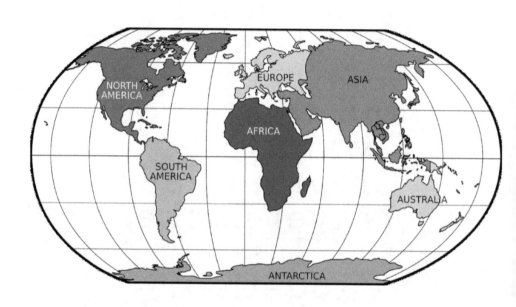

Travel Trivia:
How much do you know about the continents and countries of our planet?
Let's test your geography.

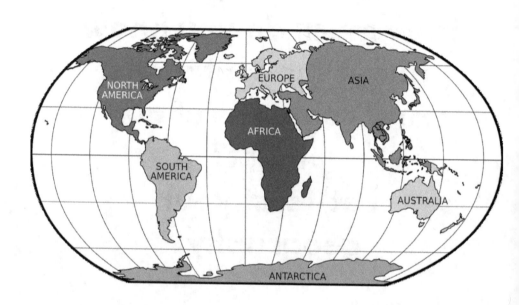

How many continents in the world?

List of the 7 continents:

NORTH AMERICA

SOUTH AMERICA

EUROPE

AFRICA

AUSTRALIA

ASIA

ANTARTICA

ANSWER:
DEPENDING ON WHAT SCHOOL OF THOUGHT
YOU SUBSCRIBE TO SEVERAL ANSWERS
COULD BE CORRECT:
BUT FOR THIS BOOK WE WILL USE

WHICH IS TRADITIONALLY TAUGHT IN
ENGLISH SPEAKING COUNTRIES.

ASIA   AFRICA   NORTH
AMERICA

SOUTH
AMERICA   EUROPE

AUSTRALIA

ANTARTICA

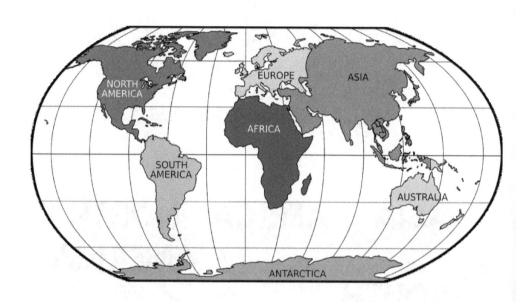

How many countries in the world?

250

150

87

165

180

195

389

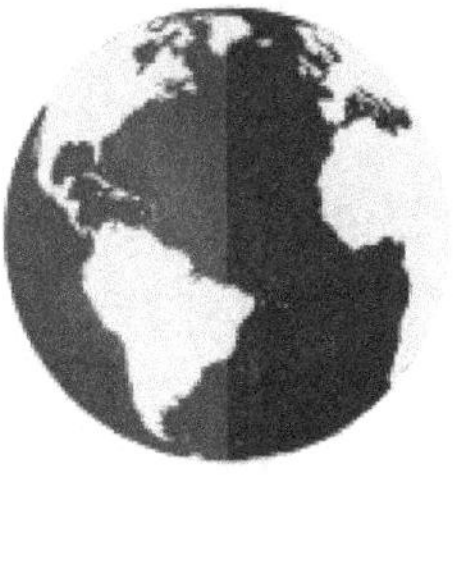

ANSWER:
AGAIN. DEPENDING ON WHAT SCHOOL OF
THOUGHT YOU SUBSCRIBE TO SEVERAL
ANSWERS COULD BE CORRECT:
BUT FOR THIS BOOK WE WILL USE THE 2019
UNITED NATIONS COUNT 193 COUNTRIES
THAT ARE MEMBER STATES OF THE UNITED
NATIONS AND 2 COUNTRIES THAT ARE NON-
MEMBER OBSERVER STATES: THE HOLY
SEE AND THE STATE OF PALESTINE.

195

Of the 7 continents and the 195 countries, do you know how many you have stepped foot on?

As a couple, use the Country/Continent Log Book in Section 2 to list each country and each continent you discover together. Write the date, country, and continent. As you travel keep it updated.

List of all the countries
in the world:

A
Afghanistan
Albania
Algeria
Andorra
Angola
Antigua and Barbuda
Argentina
Armenia
Aruba
Australia
Austria
Azerbaijan
B
Bahamas, The
Bahrain
Bangladesh
Barbados
Belarus
Belgium
Belize
Benin
Bhutan
Bolivia
Bosnia and
Herzegovina
Botswana
Brazil
Brunei
Bulgaria
Burkina Faso
Burma
Burundi

C
Cambodia
Cameroon
Canada
Cabo Verde
Central African
Republic
Chad
Chile
China
Colombia
Comoros
Congo, Democratic
Republic of the
Congo, Republic of the
Costa Rica
Cote d'Ivoire
Croatia
Cuba
Curacao
Cyprus
Czechia
D
Denmark
Djibouti
Dominica
Dominican Republic
E
East Timor (see Timor-
Leste)
Ecuador
Egypt
El Salvador
Equatorial Guinea
Eritrea
Estonia
Ethiopia

F
Fiji
Finland
France
G
Gabon
Gambia The
Georgia
Germany
Ghana
Greece
Grenada
Guatemala
Guinea
Guinea-Bissau
Guyana
H
Haiti
Holy See
Honduras
Hong Kong
Hungary
I
Iceland
India
Indonesia
Iran
Iraq
Ireland
Israel
Italy
J
Jamaica
Japan
Jordan
K
Kazakhtan
Kenya

K

Kiribati
Korea, North
Korea, South
Kosovo
Kuwait
Kyrgyzstan

L

Laos
Latvia
Lebanon
Lesotho
Liberia
Libya
Liechtenstein
Lithuania
Luxembourg

M

Macau
Macedonia
Madagascar
Malawi
Malaysia
Maldives
Mali
Malta
Marshall Islands
Mauritania
Mauritius
Mexico
Micronesia
Moldova
Monaco
Mongolia
Montenegro
Morocco
Mozambique

N
Namibia
Nauru
Nepal
Netherlands
New Zealand
Nicaragua
Niger
Nigeria
North Korea
Norway
O
Oman
P
Pakistan
Palau
Palestinian Territories
Panama
Papua New Guinea
Paraguay
Peru
Philippines
Poland
Portugal
Q
Qatar
R
Romania
Russia
Rwanda
S
Saint Kitts and Nevis
Saint Lucia
Saint Vincent and the
Grenadines
Samoa

S

Sao Tome and Principe
Saudi Arabia
Senegal
Serbia
Seychelles
Sierra Leone
Singapore
Sint Maarten
Slovakia
Slovenia
Solomon Islands
Somalia
South Africa
South Korea
South Sudan
Spain
Sri Lanka
Sudan
Suriname
Swaziland
Sweden
Switzerland
Syria

T

Taiwan
Tajikistan
Tanzania
Thailand
Timor-Leste
Togo
Tonga
Trinidad and Tobago
Tunisia
Turkey
Turkmenistan
Tuvalu

U
Uganda
Ukraine
United Arab Emirates
United Kingdom
Uruguay
Uzbekistan
V
Vanuatu
Venezuela
Vietnam

Y
Yemen
Z
Zambia
Zimbabwe

Circle the countries you want to visit.
Look up the ones you never heard of.
Write down the ones you visited in Section 2. Pick
one country that is the
road less traveled and have an adventure of a
lifetime.

The list of countries can differ from different
sources. This list is from:

The U.S. Department of State.
https://www.state.gov/misc/list/index.htm

List of the 7 continents:

Circle the ones you have
visited and write the countries
you would most like to see
under each continent.

North America

South America

Europe

Asia

Australia

Antarctica

Africa

Life is too short, make your list and get busy living.

Take this Travel Quiz and compare your answers with your partner:

Do you think you like the same type of vacations?

Answer the questions individually, then see how many answers you have in common.

This exercise will help you make a bucket list you both will enjoy.

Quiz: What kind of traveler are you?
Take the following quiz. Answer the questions as an individual. Score to find out what kind of traveler you are.
Compare answers as a couple.

1. In my mind, the word vacation conjures up an image that fits in one of these categories:
   a. Beach scene, island, tropical
   b. Skyscrapers, vibrant city scene, fantastic food
   c. Woods, forest, trails, trees
   d. Landmarks, old castles, museums, history
2. If I had to choose one of the following activities to do on my vacation, I would choose:
   a. A lounge chair, blue water, a good book, a frozen cocktail
   b. Sightseeing, trains, night clubs, shopping
   c. Hiking, skiing, camping, biking
   d. Tours to little known places, art, history, knowledge
3. You scored a free vacation, which one would you pick?
   a. All-inclusive resort vacation in Turks and Caicos
   b. 4 nights in Manhattan, with show tickets
   c. An RV for a week in Colorado
   d. A European guided tour of castles.
4. Which type of movie/series do you most want to watch?
   a. Bay Watch, Fools Gold, Secret islands of the world. or Cocktail
   b. Sex and the City, Man on the Ledge, Foodie City Style
   c. Into the Wild, The Edge, The Great Outdoors, Everest
   d. Downton Abbey, The Da Vinci Code, The History channel
5. Pick a song out of the following you would like to hear right now:
   a. No Shoes No Shirt No problem
   b. New York New York
   c. Take me Home Country Road
   d. Brahms Symphony No 1

6. What do you most feel like packing on a trip?
   a. Bathing suits, shorts, t-shirts, flip flops, beachy dresses
   b. Fly clothes, club clothes, clothes that make a statement
   c. hiking boots, shorts, hats, jeans, outdoor wear
   d. Comfortable clothes, walking shoes, things that pack well
7. Pick a food that sounds good to you in this moment:
   a. Shrimp, fish, fresh fruit, tropical salads, lobster
   b. Tapas, foie gras, steak, eclectic dishes, sashimi
   c. Hamburgers, hotdogs, grilled steaks, barbeque
   d. Local dishes, chocolate, Indian food, German schnitzel
8. Pick a drink you would like to order:
   a. Margarita, frozen cocktail, island local beer
   b. Cosmopolitan, champagne, Harvey wall banger,
   c. Beer, vodka, wine
   d. Pilsner, tea, coffee, port
9. Would you rather?
   a. Sit on a lounge chair listening to the waves
   b. Read your newspaper in the middle of a city outdoor café
   c. Stretch out on a blanket in the middle of the woods
   d. Eat lunch at a café in the middle of an Art Museum

Count 1 for every a, b, c, d, you have:

A = _____

B = _____

C = _____

D = _____

Count 1 for every a, b, c, d, you have:

A = _____

B = _____

C = _____

D = _____

Answers:

A- If you have 6-9 A's, Hello beach lover. Islands, tropical weather & toes in the sand sounds like a great vacation to you. Pick an island you have never stepped foot on and go!

B- If you have 6-9 B's, you thrive in the city. People watching, night life and the energy of the crowds wake you up. Check out a city center you have never visited and immerse yourself in the city.

C- If you scored 6-9 C's, you are a back to nature kind of person. Explore the off the beaten track places. Hike to somewhere most people never see in their lifetime.

D- If you scored 6-9 D's, you love history. You seek out places that tell a story, locations that shed light on where we came from. Check out a medieval city, or a city in the national historic registry.

3-5 A's, you like the beach, it's on your list, but you like to mix it up with a variety of vacations.

3-5 B's, you enjoy the city. but you like variety & change

3-5 C's, you love nature and off the beaten track but not all the time.

3-5 D's, History is fascinating to you, and you want to explore a slice of it on your vacation.

1-2 A's, the beach is not your first choice, but you will try a tropical vacation if your other half wants to.

1-2 B's, the city is okay for some things.

1-2 C's. You can visit nature but not please no camping.

1-2 D's, you enjoy a little history, maybe 1 museum every 2 years.

Zero A's, don't go to the beach.

Zero B's, stay away from the city for vacations.

Zero C's, stay out of the woods.

Zero D's, take a nap while your partner goes to a museum.

Okay, let's imagine
YOU win two free
airline tickets…
But to use them, you must pick
a destination right now.
Shout the location (anywhere in
the world).
What destination did you
shout?
Try this one together with
your partner, set a 30-
second timer and shout
the destination.
Are your dream
destinations similar?

I picture us here someday:

Write down 4 places you can picture the two of you together. Have your partner write down four places.

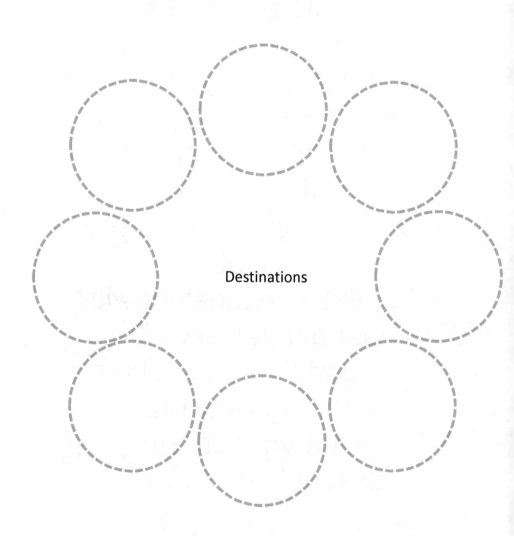

Destinations

Sometimes, I want to escape all the stress and go here: Name 3 places:

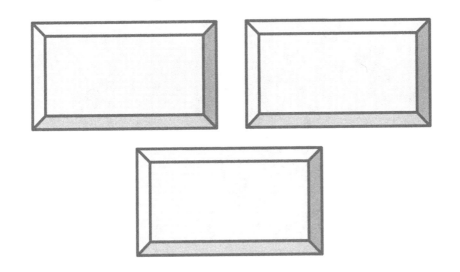

Sometimes, I want to escape all the stress and go here: Name 3 places:

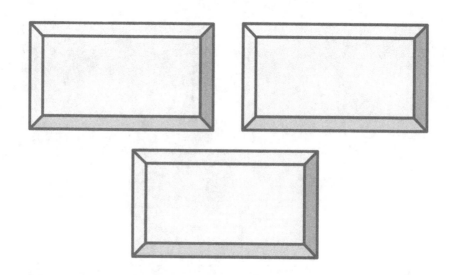

TOP 5 PLACES TO SEE

Have you discovered some similarities in your top destinations?

TOP 5 PLACES TO SEE

Have you discovered some similarities in your top destinations?

Let's think about

The places we dream of:

Brainstorm and write them all
over the page:

(Compare your answers)

Let's think about

The places we dream of:

Brainstorm and write them all
over the page:

(Compare your answers)

Pick a letter in the alphabet, any letter. Look at the list of 195 countries and pick a country to go see under that letter, pick one!

Brainstorm: Think about the top 10 places you would like to visit in the United States:

Write them down:

Brainstorm: Think about the top 5 places you would like to visit in the Central America

Write them down:

Brainstorm: Think about the top 5 places you would like to visit in Africa:

Write them down:

Brainstorm: Think about the top 10 places you would like to visit in Europe:

Write them down:

Brainstorm: Think about the top 10 places you would like to visit in Asia:

Write them down:

Brainstorm: Think about the top 10 places you would like to visit in Australia/New Zealand/New Caledonia:

Write them down:

Brainstorm: Think about the top 10 places to explore in a day's drive:

Write them down:

Brainstorm: Think about favorite
childhood vacations
(compare your answers):

Why did you love them?

If you need to escape, go somewhere together off-the-beaten-path. List obscure places you might want to try:

Now that you both did a little soul searching, try creating an initial travel bucket list.

Begin by creating a bucket list of 5 items individually and then in the Section 2 you can figure out a combined one or several lists together.

A travel bucket list is a place to begin. Change it as many times as you want.

Continue to go through this section, write your ideas, scribble, doodle.
Inspire each other.

Someday you will have a record of all your travel dreams and journeys together.

Top 10 places

Our Travel Bucket List

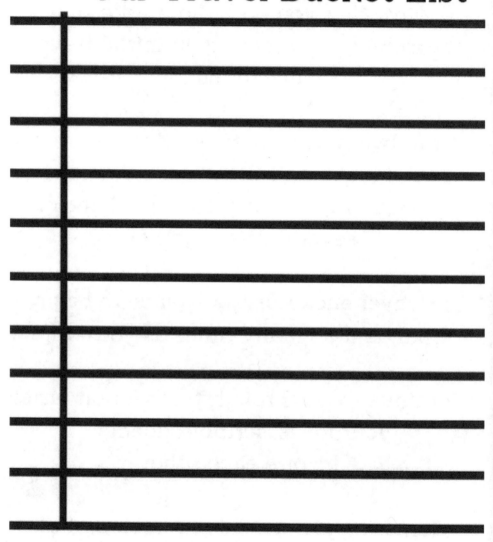

OUR TRAVEL BUCKET LIST

	✓

Adventure Awaits.

Tired of hotel rooms? Want a home away from home?
Try Airbnb.
Airbnb is a favorite way to travel. It's more than just a bed and bathroom. Experience a destination like a local. I have stayed in an oceanfront condo in the Dominican Republic, a beach house in Santa Cruz, CA, a loft in Knoxville, TN, a historic farmhouse in Western Pennsylvania, and many more. Every rental has been awesome.

If you have never used Airbnb, use this code on a first-time reservation and receive $40 off. (Airbnb can change this offer at any time and is only for first time users of Airbnb.)

For $40 off first reservation. copy this link in your browser and sign up: **www.airbnb.com/c/anitak103**

So where do you want to go next?

"Life is either a daring

adventure or nothing."

-- Helen Keller

Jot down some notes on a destination you have heard about, but know nothing about. Do some research on Google. Watch a movie filmed in that location or read a book with the setting in that area.

As soon as I saw you, I knew our life together would be an adventure we would never forget.

Anita Kaltenbaugh

"The World is a book and those who do not travel read only a page." – Saint Augustine

I haven't been everywhere,
but it sounds
like a great place.

Remember to take time to pause, and live in the moment.

Sometimes we just need to say "Yes" more often...

"The journey not
the arrival matters."
–T.S. Eliot

Imagine, you found a magic bottle and a travel genie popped out granting you three vacations, anywhere in the world? Where would you choose?

1.

2.

3.

"Once a year, go
someplace you've
never been before."
– Dalai Lama

Though we travel the world over to find the beautiful, we must carry it with us, or we find it not.
Ralph Waldo Emerson

If we were meant to stay in one place, we'd have roots instead of feet. -unknown

Life teaches us many things,
but travel with
someone you love and
you'll know if you're meant
to be together...

The sea lives in every one of us. -Wyland

Write out seaside locations you want to see:

"You only live once, but if you do it right, once is enough." --*Mae West*

Write your top 2 travel destinations
on a piece
of paper.
include your email address and your
name,
Write, "This is where we want to
Travel to…"
Roll it up, place it in a bottle
and …wait for it…don't toss it out to sea.
It will probably end up in a floating garbage dump.

So, instead …hide it somewhere you
might find it in the future, or where
someone else might discover it.

Who knows…when you see it years later, maybe your
travel dreams came true.

And we will travel
together
And just be in love
Forever -unknown

Sometimes the best
anniversary present is taking a
trip together.

Travel far enough, and you may find out who you really are.

A.K. Smith

Ebook is <u>Free on KU</u>

Here's a book with INSIDER SECRETS to save money and get you taking more vacations by understanding tips and tricks to afford traveling.

Travel Secrets: Insider guide to planning, affording and taking more vacations by Anita Kaltenbaugh

Go see the world.

Traveling it leaves you speechless, then turns you into a storyteller.
IBN BATTUTA

"It does not matter how slowly you go, so long as you do not stop." *Confucious*

"Learn from yesterday, live for today, hope for tomorrow. The important thing is not to stop questioning."
-- *Albert Einstein*

Traveling makes one **modest,** you see the tiny space **you** occupy in the **world. –**

Gustave Flaubert

The world is big and I want to
get a good look at it before it
gets dark.
- John Muir
Where do you want to go
before it gets dark?

Why travel?

Why breathe or exist...Travel outside your box and open your mind and heart.

Get away from it all or get into it all.

If you schedule vacations like doctor appointments, you will be healthier.

Open your mind and see the world.

Just go.

If you need to escape, go somewhere together off-the-beaten-path. List obscure places you might want to try:

How do you know if you like this or that if you've never tried it?
Write a list of places you wonder if you would like, then do some research.

Have you thought of 3 new places you might want to see? Write them down.

"He who does not travel does not know the value of men."
Moorish proverb

We watched a movie that was filmed in this location and now we want to go here:

Fact:
If you never plan to get away, you won't go.

Plan your vacations together
and they will happen.
Get excited about the
upcoming trip. Use post-it
notes to make a countdown on
your bathroom mirror.

Only put off until tomorrow what you are willing to die having left undone."
-*Pablo Picasso*

Bid on a travel auction. It might be the one destination you didn't even know you were supposed to visit.

(tip: try Luxury Link or Google travel auctions, if you are flexible you can snag a deal 40% -60% off)

Pick a weekend once a month and getaway, even if it's close by.

If I won an all expense paid vacation I would choose...

(Compare your answers, are they similar?)

See the world, maybe even the moon.

Notes from a wonderful trip:

Adventure is worthwhile
- Aesop

I want to use this mode of transportation on my next trip:

We travel not to escape life, but for life
to escape us

-unknown

In my mind I see myself in this exotic location?

Where?

What's your favorite
Season?
Pick a location that is in
that season and plan a
trip.
Go to a place with the
weather you love...
write down a few ideas:

Surprise the one you love with
a trip. A weekend get-away.
Plan it. Pack for them. Don't
tell them or give it away.
Blindfolds are a great touch.
Create an authentic surprise.
Make a memory.
Make sure to write it down in
the back of this book.

Take me:

To move, to breathe, to fly, to float, to roam the roads of lands remote, to travel is to live.

Hans Christian Andersen

Travel Notes:

DATE

Section 2: Travel logs, records and bucket lists.

Always take the scenic route

Countries & Continents

DATE | PLACE

Countries & Continents

DATE	PLACE

Countries & Continents

Countries & Continents

DATE · PLACE

Our Travel Bucket List

Travel Memories:

Hotel/Motel/Lodging Dream Destinations:

Unique accommodations

Travel Memories:

OUR TRAVEL BUCKET LIST

	✓

Make a plan.
Otherwise it's all talk.

Die with memories
not dreams
- unknown

Use the following pages to log every
vacation, adventure, journey and voyage you have taken
together.
Write the date, place and your favorite memory of the trip.

Log of our
travels:

	DATE:
	STATE/COUNTRY

	DATE:
	STATE/COUNTRY

	DATE:
	STATE/COUNTRY

Where we stayed/favorite moment

	DATE:
	STATE/COUNTRY
	DATE:
	STATE/COUNTRY
	DATE:
	STATE/COUNTRY
	DATE:
	STATE/COUNTRY
	DATE:
	STATE/COUNTRY
	DATE DUE
	STATE/COUNTRY
	DATE DUE
	STATE/COUNTRY
	DATE DUE
	STATE/COUNTRY
	DATE DUE
	STATE/COUNTRY

Where we stayed/favorite moment:

DATE:

STATE/COUNTRY

DATE:

STATE/COUNTRY

DATE:

STATE/COUNTRY

DATE:

STATE/COUNTRY

Where we stayed/favorite moment

	DATE:
	STATE/COUNTRY
	DATE:
	STATE/COUNTRY
	DATE:
	STATE/COUNTRY
	DATE:
	STATE/COUNTRY
	DATE:
	STATE/COUNTRY
	DATE DUE
	STATE/COUNTRY
	DATE DUE
	STATE/COUNTRY
	DATE DUE
	STATE/COUNTRY
	DATE DUE
	STATE/COUNTRY

Where we stayed/favorite moment:

	DATE: STATE/COUNTRY
	DATE: STATE/COUNTRY
	DATE: STATE/COUNTRY
	DATE: STATE/COUNTRY

Where we stayed/favorite moment

	DATE:
	STATE/COUNTRY
	DATE:
	STATE/COUNTRY
	DATE:
	STATE/COUNTRY
	DATE:
	STATE/COUNTRY
	DATE:
	STATE/COUNTRY
	DATE DUE
	STATE/COUNTRY
	DATE DUE
	STATE/COUNTRY
	DATE DUE
	STATE/COUNTRY
	DATE DUE
	STATE/COUNTRY

Where we stayed/favorite moment:

DATE:

STATE/COUNTRY

DATE:

STATE/COUNTRY

DATE:

STATE/COUNTRY

DATE:

STATE/COUNTRY

Where we stayed/favorite moment

	DATE:
	STATE/COUNTRY
	DATE:
	STATE/COUNTRY
	DATE:
	STATE/COUNTRY
	DATE:
	STATE/COUNTRY
	DATE:
	STATE/COUNTRY
	DATE DUE
	STATE/COUNTRY
	DATE DUE
	STATE/COUNTRY
	DATE DUE
	STATE/COUNTRY
	DATE DUE
	STATE/COUNTRY

Where we stayed/favorite moment:

DATE:

STATE/COUNTRY

DATE:

STATE/COUNTRY

DATE:

STATE/COUNTRY

DATE:

STATE/COUNTRY

Where we stayed/favorite moment

	DATE:
	STATE/COUNTRY
	DATE:
	STATE/COUNTRY
	DATE:
	STATE/COUNTRY
	DATE:
	STATE/COUNTRY
	DATE:
	STATE/COUNTRY
	DATE DUE
	STATE/COUNTRY
	DATE DUE
	STATE/COUNTRY
	DATE DUE
	STATE/COUNTRY
	DATE DUE
	STATE/COUNTRY

Where we stayed/favorite moment:

DATE:

STATE/COUNTRY

DATE:

STATE/COUNTRY

DATE:

STATE/COUNTRY

DATE:

STATE/COUNTRY

Travel Notes:

Travel Notes:

For more inspirational journals or milestones gift visit:
www.bookswithsoul.com
and for travel reviews on places to go:
http://www.wordstravelfilm.com

Who knows what will happen to our data in the future?

Celebrate the art of writing by choosing to pen your words on paper.

Check out _Books With Soul_
Bookswithsoul.com
Your Words. Your Pages.
Like us on Facebook
Bookswithsoulamazon

ABOUT THE AUTHOR

Books with Soul believes in sharing gifts that inspire and motivate others to create memories and keep a record of the story of their life.

What if… you had a record of your memories or someone you loved?

INSPIRATION COMES IN ALL SIZES, SHAPES AND IDEAS

WE believe every life is worth a few written words to pass on or reflect on in the future.

You don't have to be an author to tell the story of your life. Just be you.

Books with Soul ™was inspired from a lover of music and life, who believed in the soul. He had a collection of wonderful things. Physical memories you could read, touch, and listen to-including thousands of vinyl albums. Old school music, that lasts forever. In 2018, he passed away from brain cancer, but his memory lives on as others go old school. Collect pieces of your history, put pencil to paper, and record written memories. A physical book will not be lost in the cloud and will last longer than a lifetime.

Keep a record of the story of your life. Your Words. Your Pages.
This is for you Mark.

Buy a journal from bookswithsoul.com and write your story.

Also Available on Amazon from Books with Soul:
Just Breathe
Words I Want to Say
Every Breath-A Journal of Gratitude and Blessings
Remember When
Travel Journal-My Travel Bucket List
WISH- how to make my wishes come true
Ramblings of a Crazy Pregnant Women
Camp Memories
Reflections from the Beach
Gratitude Journal: I Can Only Imagine: 52 weeks
The Plan
Reflections of My Life- and things I want to remember
25th Anniversary: Twenty five Epic Years
Hunters Journal: Hunting Season
Just do it Journal: I'd Pick More Daisies
I was here: a travel log of everywhere I've been and where I'm going.
Reflections of the Beach
The Art of Possibility
Seriously I'm 50? My drink & advice book: 50 Drink recipes
Dirt Road Diaries: My off-road adventures
Remember When? Guest book
My little book I write shit down in
Old Soul: Blank Notebook for ideas and sketching
Music Journal: My Music Journey

I would like to travel the world with you twice.
Once to see the world. Twice, to see the way you see
the world.
– unknown

The Adventures of Us

CPSIA information can be obtained
at www.ICGtesting.com
Printed in the USA
LVHW082333140220
647074LV00005B/20